CONTE

C000062534

CHOICE

David Morley • *FURY* • Carcanet Press

RECOMMENDATIONS

Sean Borodale • *Inmates* • Cape Poetry
Kate Miller • *The Long Beds* • Carcanet Press
Nina Mingya Powles • *Magnolia, 木蘭* • Nine Arches Press
Mervyn Taylor • *Country of Warm Snow* • Shearsman

SPECIAL COMMENDATION

Gerður Kristný • *Reykjavik Requiem* • Arc Publications

RECOMMENDED TRANSLATIONS

Mesándel Virtusio Arguelles • *Three Books* • Broken Sleep Books
Translated by Kristine Ong Muslim
10 Contemporary Spanish Women Poets • Shearsman • Trans. Terence Dooley

WORLD CHOICE

I Am A Rohingya • Arc Publications • Edited by James Byrne and Shehzar Doja

PAMPHLET CHOICE

Cheryl Pearson • *Menagerie* • The Emma Press

WILD CARD

Rachel Long • *My Darling From the Lions* • Picador

Poetry Book Society

CHOICE SELECTORS RECOMMENDATION SPECIAL COMMENDATION	SINÉAD MORRISSEY & ANDREW McMILLAN
TRANSLATION SELECTOR	ILYA KAMINSKY
PAMPHLET SELECTORS	MARY JEAN CHAN & NICK MAKOHA
WILD CARD SELECTOR	ANTHONY ANAXAGOROU
CONTRIBUTORS	SOPHIE O'NEILL NATHANIEL SPAIN
EDITORIAL & DESIGN	ALICE KATE MULLEN

Main Poetry Book Society Memberships
Choice
4 Books a Year: 4 Choice books & 4 *Bulletins* a year (UK £55, Europe £65, ROW £75)
World
8 Books: 4 Choices, 4 Translation books & 4 *Bulletins* (£98, £120, £132)
Charter
20 Books: 4 Choices, 16 Recommendations and 4 *Bulletins* (£180, £210, £235)
Complete
24 Books: 4 Choices, 16 Recommendations, 4 Translations, 4 *Bulletins* (£223, £265, £292)

Single copies of the *Bulletin* £9.99

Cover Art Sophie Herxheimer, poetryteapot.wordpress.com

Copyright Poetry Book Society and contributors. All rights reserved.
ISBN 9781913129194 ISSN 0551-1690

Poetry Book Society | Milburn House | Dean Street | Newcastle upon Tyne | NE1 1LF
0191 230 8100 | enquiries@poetrybooksociety.co.uk

WWW.POETRYBOOKS.CO.UK

LETTER FROM THE PBS

Somehow it is Autumn. We hope that you and your families are keeping well and we really hope that the Poetry Book Society and the poetry we share has helped you through the last few months – we truly believe in the power of poetry to heal and connect, so a big WELCOME to new members and many thanks to those returning!

Our Autumn *Bulletin* cover continues our series celebration of poet-artists and we're honoured to feature this vibrant new artwork created during lockdown by the artist and poet Sophie Herxheimer. 'Yellow Flowers Multiply at a Greater Speed Even than Viral Droplets' is a colourful reminder that nature, creativity and hope continue to thrive, even in the toughest of circumstances.

This quarter's Choice is the magnificent *FURY* by David Morley, he writes, "The characters in my book are voiceless but powerful... These are their poems". This season's selections sit beautifully alongside one another and the theme of giving voice to the voiceless features in many of the collections. The selections offer a call to come together, to respect nature and all language, to give dignity and life and pay homage to the ignored or oppressed.

A warm welcome to Sinéad Morrissey, this *Bulletin* is Sinéad's first set of selections and commentaries with Andrew McMillan. I'd also like to introduce our inaugural World Choice, awarded to an outstanding collection of non-European poetry or translation published within the last five years, selected by Ilya Kaminsky.

We are delighted to see so many of our selections featured in the Forward Prizes shortlists, and so pleased that Regi Claire, winner of our PBS & Mslexia Women's Poetry Prize is on the shortlist for best single poem. Like last year we're offering a special Forward Prizes bundle at a discounted rate for PBS members. Our virtual events are also continuing – if you haven't attended the Insta Live Book Club hosted by Andrew McMillan (or watched at your leisure on our YouTube channel) please do come along. It's a brilliant hour of live poetry discussion and interviews with our selected poets. You can also watch our virtual PBS Showcase readings by Nina Mingya Powles and Rachel Long at Cheltenham Literature Festival on the 9th October and Bhanu Kapil at Durham Book Festival on the 14th October. Visit www.poetrybooks.co.uk for more details. As ever, we love to hear from you so please do get in touch with your comments!

SOPHIE O'NEILL
PBS & INPRESS DIRECTOR

DAVID MORLEY

David Morley is an ecologist and naturalist. He studied Zoology at the University of Bristol and pursued research on acid rain. His poetry has won a Gregory Award, the Ted Hughes Award, and a Cholmondeley Award. He was elected a Fellow of the Royal Society of Literature in 2018. His Carcanet collections include *The Magic of What's There*, *The Invisible Gift*, *The Gypsy and the Poet*, *Enchantment*, *The Invisible Kings*, and *Scientific Papers*. He is also known for poetry installations in natural landscapes, and podcasts on Creative Writing. David is a professor at Warwick University and Monash University. His work in education has been awarded a National Teaching Fellowship.

FURY

CARCANET PRESS | £10.99 | PBS PRICE   £8.25

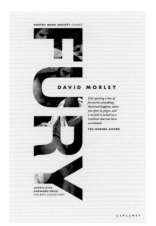

In *FURY*, the speaker of the poem 'Gypsies' asserts: "All the nameless people named here. / The story ends with who we were." Epitaph, epigraph, mirror, this couplet pivots on Morley's running preoccupations: speaking out/up for others (which he accompanies with scrupulous self-regard), the magic and pitfalls of narrative; a protean 'I' voice, and a masterful deployment of language and form. Similar feats of naming and voice-throwing populate *FURY*, from the dramatic monologues of Tyson Fury and a mythical Gypsy key-cutter, to the epic 'The Caravans of Tarshish' which names – over twenty-three rolling pages – the attendees at the funeral of "The Prince of the Gypsies" Wisdom Smith in 1839, including "and of the Throstles   Only Mad Throstle" and "Damage and Atonement of the Mountains / Deedrik and Antichrist of the Sansoms". In true Shamanic fashion, to name is to reanimate, and to reanimate is to become: past and present, I, you, they – all are conjured and held together, transmuted by poetry.

In *FURY*, Morley's concerns combine as never before into a keening, politicised call to pay attention to the missing, the lost, and the deliberately elided: the Roma Holocaust or *Porajmos* ("The Devouring"); the destruction of the Dale Farm Traveller Camp; the ongoing incarceration of Towfiq Bihani in Guantánamo Bay. Morley, a Natural Scientist and Ecologist, also urges us to watch out for the animals with whom we share this planet, while we still can, and is a brilliantly sonic writer of birds, in particular. Morley's trademark fusion of Romani and English – "Angloromani" – forges afresh his lyric gifts, from the rainbow-burst of 'She is Leaf-like and Bird-like', to the searing elegy 'After the Burial of the Gypsy Matriarch'. By holding two languages, two world-views and two ways of existing in symmetry, such poems double the very texture of the world.

Translations From A Stammerer
after a phrase by Anna Akhmatova

I like owl-lamps to be left burning in each room,
bedroom doors ajar after owl-dark,
the hearth-fire hooting like an owl up the chimney.

You lift and light the lantern of an owl,
open the owl-door, switch on the owl-light.
The garden flickers with filaments of owl-flight.

SINÉAD MORRISSEY

DAVID MORLEY

Ted Hughes wrote, "It's my suspicion that no poem can be a poem that is not a statement from the powers in control of our life, the ultimate suffering and decision in us." The powers that control us – our Furies – can be merciless. The decision in us, if speech will allow, gives voice to those powers. The characters in my book are voiceless but powerful: Gypsies, detainees, fighters. I love them and feel close to their characters, to people I know and have grown with. I laughed and wept with them, as friends. I took them at their word without taking their words.

These are their poems. There are poems that flare from terror and fold into redemption. There are poems of self-wrought tragedy answered by remarkable love. Each poem in the book weighs the other, in language and sound. The arrangement of the poems, the arcing of the book, required a lot of feeling-through and listening. I regard a book as a form of poetry, even of music. And *FURY* found its voices within a book's long-flowing form. Fury is a form of expression: the fury of creation.

One of the spurs behind my becoming a poet is my stammer, which I write about through a sequence of translated poets. My stammer has been a Fury. Spoken word is after all at the heart of my poetry, and indeed most poetry. I have never spoken aloud without being aware of impossibility: speech as suffering and shame. My mind developed into a thesaurus of synonyms to find the path of least resistance through forests of words. I became a Lyrebird of language. And this book is where my blessed and cursed Furies speak together, in English and Romani, in poetry and birdcalls, in silence and in song.

DAVID RECOMMENDS

Mona Arshi, *Small Hands* (Pavilion Poetry); Caroline Bird, *The Air Year* (Carcanet); Zoë Brigley, *Hand & Skull* (Bloodaxe); Mary Jean Chan, *Flèche* (Faber & Faber); Tishani Doshi, *Girls are Coming out of the Woods* (Bloodaxe); Jane Draycott, *Pearl* (Carcanet); Sarah Howe, *Loop of Jade* (Chatto & Windus); Mimi Khalvati, *Child* (Carcanet); Rachel Long, *My Darling from the Lions* (Picador); Kim Moore, *The Art of Falling* (Seren); Sinéad Morrissey, *On Balance* (Carcanet); Pascale Petit, *Mama Amazonica* (Bloodaxe); Yvonne Reddick, *Spikenard* (The Poetry Business) and Tracy K. Smith, *Life on Mars* (Graywolf).

FIRST LYREBIRD

Your vow is the Lyrebird's thesaurus of mimicry.
  Your vow yaffles with the laughter of a Kookaburra.

Your vow sings the syllables you share with our children.
  Your vow lullabies a jungle's stories, canopies, and understory.

My vow catapults a Kingfisher past a Kookaburra.
  My vow scales a frozen waterfall's icicled aviary.

My vow strips a eucalypt's paperbark for nests for Rainbow Lorys.
  My vow ploughs a ridge-walk through a peat-bog's slog and slurry.

Your vow paints Jane Austen's miniatures on two inches of ivory.
  Your vow quickens a bare forest with your footsteps in snow.

Your vow spills its watershed through the fell's tarns and freshets
  and startles snowdrops from the floor of heaven.

My vow hushes a fir forest and my footsteps in snow.
  My vow spies a single star from out the wide night's numbers.

THE THROWN VOICE

Romany

'The story starts with who you are.
I strode at night across the heath to hear
a nightjar. It was night which throws
her voice inside a bird. I would stand below
his song and become cast into creature,
into his purled world. The bird could never
be seen. It seemed a soft scar of sound
as if a lone tree's bark sang the night's wound
from a lone tree's bough, and yet heath
and bird were grown two in the dark.
Those wound, wounded voices were thrown
into me, as if bird and tree were hornbooks
I could finger and trace and sing aloud.
I spoke through night, or night through me
and all the creatures of the night sang free.
My Gypsies gave tongue to campfire stories
but my spell drew speech from the circling heath.
I was a magician to them, the magic man
to my people. I lost it. I lost my magic
when I lost those voices. I cried my eyes out.
I have cried my eyes into myself. How can
you know what it is like to lose your magic?'

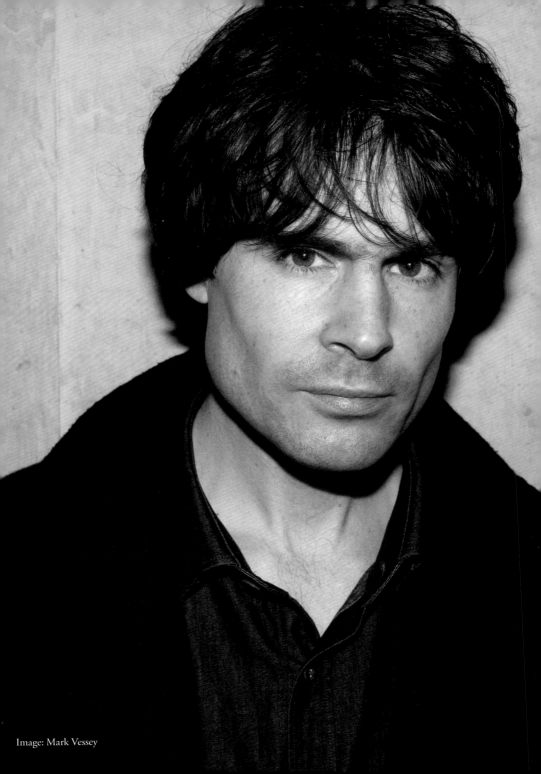

SEAN BORODALE

Sean Borodale was born in London and works as a poet and artist. His first collection of poetry *Bee Journal* was shortlisted for the 2012 Aldeburgh First Collection Prize, the Costa Poetry Book Award and the T.S. Eliot Prize. In 2014 he was selected as a Next Generation Poet. He currently teaches Creative Writing at Royal Holloway.

INMATES

CAPE POETRY | £10.00 | PBS PRICE £7.50

SEAN
BORODALE

Inmates

CAPE POETRY

The last poem of *Inmates*, 'Hot Bright Visionary Flies', ends "One day it will stop: / the air will stop; the light will stop". As if the whizzing and whirring of a populous micro-world, which Borodale has scrutinised, has suddenly been switched off and we are left with the silence of the final empty pages in which to contemplate what has happened. And the end is the point: even if not as explicitly stated elsewhere, the plight of insects in this Age of Mass Extinction, and consequently of everything else, including ourselves, haunts this collection of intense, highly-wrought lyrics, as taut within their cages of sprung words as a beetle in its shell.

In 'Death Place of a Small Tortoiseshell Under its Food Source, the Nettle', the speaker asks, "Do you forget how to look?"– whether addressed to himself, the tortoiseshell, the reader, or all three, remains unclear. In *The Art of Description*, Mark Doty argues for an ethics of attention which is viscerally present here. And I am grateful to be taught how to look again, at the "creepy jewel box", that is 'Maggots at the Back of the Cupboard', or at the "compass of hunger", the "madrigal of waiting" that is a cobweb ('Cobweb A.M.'). The possibility that all this may pass, and soon, freights each startling observation with careful urgency.

Even the self is atomised under the forensic glare of watching. In 'Hawk Moth & Queen Wasp', the speaker "drips" with his "eyes" (cries) and goes on to announce: "I do not see the outside of my head; / it is un-mirrored and in abeyance." Humans have not only caused the devastation; we are implicated, inevitably, in the apocalypse. Throughout *Inmates* Borodale ironically unites observer and observed in an appropriate and innovative language of fissured extremes.

> I drip with my eyes
> to the rupture of one, the plight of the other.
>
> My head is a lump of fist-squeezed clay.
>
> Offer them solidarity – something.
> I cannot fly, cannot make sky.
>
> The graft-line between us,
> fragile as dry grass before winter rain.

SINÉAD MORRISSEY

SEAN BORODALE

In February 2019, news reported the first global scientific review of insect populations, warning of an impending "catastrophic collapse of nature's ecosystems". *Inmates*, written in the presence of insects living and dying, did not directly start with this concern; though the book emerges in the tail-end of a year whose catastrophic Covid-19 pandemic is without doubt precipitated by human infringement upon habitats of non-human species, and a bewildering of the planet's ecosystems. *Inmates* is sadly at home in such a world. The poems, recording time spent with insects, were written in perhaps the best possible complex for studying insects, that of a young family. With its yeasts, woodlice, newts, woodworm, moulds, parents and children, the house and its innate cosmos turned about the sun, and the poems were written. As with my first collection, *Bee Journal*, which tracks epiphanies and failures in beekeeping over two years, these poems take up problems of language in proximity, through a miniature, makeshift theatre of writing in-situ. We seem to fear these very beings that are beings; who seem to serve no purpose, yet do, not merely as shadow workers within economies of tyranny.

The house as refuge – a living cell – was enlivened by those life-forms whose intricacies within the locale stretch back over infinitely vaster sequences of generation than its humans. So it is: the insect intrinsic; and the human – ill-equipped to understand such dialects of presence – the alien. These poems are not encyclopaedic, being barely informed by written texts; instead, they look, listen and try to say of where they are, and what is happening, and who might be there. Writing these poems felt like a political act: dedication to a specific kind of time towards hoped-for solidarity. I was aware of language stress, of gaps without possibility of mergence; what emerged often was the emergency behind speech. Global reports can be hard to fit to intimacies of place; yet for a global science, observations must be somehow drawn from specific instances in every locale. These poems are about trying to speak of "in situ", of shared life in tenures of relationships, of which insects are an essence.

SEAN RECOMMENDS

Zaffar Kunial, *Us* (Faber); Doireann Ní Ghríofa, *Clasp* (Dedalus); Fiona Benson, *Vertigo & Ghost* (Cape); Paul Farley, *The Mizzy* (Picador); Tishani Doshi, *Girls Are Coming Out of the Woods* (Bloodaxe); Raymond Antrobus, *The Perseverance* (Penned in the Margins); Francis Ponge, *The Table* (Wakefield Press); Carolyn Forché, *In the Lateness of the World* (Bloodaxe); Kristin Chang, *Past Lives, Future Bodies* (Black Lawrence Press) and Danez Smith, *Don't Call Us Dead* (Chatto).

a winged rubble
of momentum

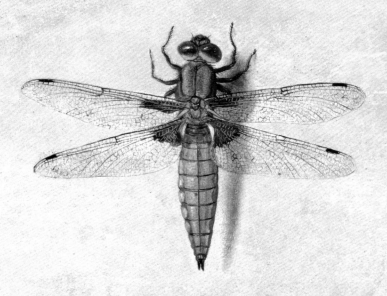

BEES & THISTLES

Thistles, three foot, four;
towers of flower-crown, tin shelter,
bleeding black feet;
not any other language, but bleeding feet.
Not collateral or nuance,
but manacled, scratched.
Until it is bees, not thistles,
along edges and tips of sticks;
her intelligence his,
his hers
until end-games of nectaries;
then nothing
but detached wing,
air stained with humming.

Image: Alison Romanczuk

KATE MILLER

Kate Miller is an award-winning poet and recipient of the Edwin Morgan International Poetry Prize in 2008. Her debut *The Observances* (2015) was shortlisted for the Costa and Michael Murphy Prizes and won the Seamus Heaney Centre Prize for First Collection. Trained in Art History and Fine Art, her teaching career in the arts was enlivened by creative collaborations, performances and site specific installations. Events she devised for the Hayward Gallery focussed on light and colour on the Thames which later led to a 2016 commission to celebrate Waterloo Bridge. As a writer and in her doctoral research, she examines perceptions of the shoreline of rivers and beaches, of what is cast up and can be reclaimed – bringing history and memory to a sense of place. She lives in South London and on the Isle of Oxney with her family.

RECOMMENDATION

THE LONG BEDS

CARCANET | £10.99 | PBS PRICE £8.25

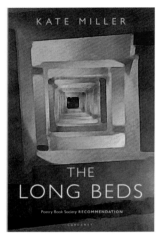

Kate Miller's second collection *The Long Beds* exists within a deep fold between the twin pages of sleeping and waking. These aren't anecdotal poems about normal life, nor do they offer a recounting of dreams (which so rarely work in poetry), they exist instead in that odd, liminal space between the two. 'Outside the Mind Shop', which opens the collection, could actually be a useful phrase to frame the whole book – outside of the rational mind and yet not in any concrete place we might recognise; Hughes, Oswald and Shakespeare all float quietly in and out of this poem too.

> ...My bed's an island
> where I've *cried to dream again*
>
> beside the ones who once lay close to me,
> the nearest. If I could only sleep and hear them speak.
>
> But in the dark outside the Mind Shop
> foxes must be tearing into stuff

Elsewhere, what might be a straightforward consideration of what the title calls the 'locomotion of laundry', becomes fresh, gets made surreal, because of the precision and peculiarity of the language: "Bedding, always being displaced, you could say / exiled, forms a line of bundles, refugees." The sea is a recurring motif throughout the collection (in that Matthew Arnold sense, that its "unplumb'd... estranging"), and other things like boats return again and again as well.

Art is a constant feature of these poems, but on reading this collection, one is struck too by the idea of a symphony, in which images, like notes, are returned to, but are reshaped and remade each time.

Beneath the surface of even the seemingly safest of poems, there is something lurking, almost as in old folk tales, a danger or a disquiet which is never far away. This feels particularly true in the titular poem 'The Long Beds', but could be said of so many poems in this collection. It's a collection which is always shifting its voice, its gaze, its locations. Almost like a riptide, the sleeping and waking worlds pulling in different directions, these are the poems which come in between, which rise up to the surface.

ANDREW McMILLAN

KATE MILLER

What are the long beds? Rafts of sleepers floating in the early morning on a stretch of water I did not recognise until the book began to form around the vision and I visited the place where I grew up and knew it. Still vaguer were echoes from my grandmother's evocation of India, a lost landscape surfacing and touching me through layers of the past without a sense of the passage of time – which is like dreaming.

Landscapes, made poignant by departure, seem embedded in a part of my perception that opens up at night. Out of the "racing cinematics of our bed, theatre of insomnia" (note from diary, 2017) I salvage what I can, transcribing waking thoughts, trying to untangle memories and old longings.

I notice the horizontality or frieze-like quality of many compositions as they unroll, that mix of long and short perspectives typical of being recumbent – "deserter", said Virginia Woolf, "from the army of the upright" – scanning the sky or ceiling, mapping the contours and close grain of grass or bedding.

In Art, beds stand for the somatic and private. More enigmatic than a royal tomb or painted bed scene, Tracey Emin's empty bed, Rachel Whiteread's casts of mattresses stir strong responses in me. There's the materiality, the literalness of bed itself, that plinth where we lie, cementing our bonds and affairs, taking comfort, bearing separation: wedlock, childbed, deathbed. "Our responsibilities did not begin / in dreams, though they began in bed" – Frank O'Hara.

My own experience of the long bed was of solitary confinement in hospital, fevered and hallucinating. Convalescing, I read wonderful writing on illness, solitude, sleep and our need to dream. Thus, in the late stages of editing this book, when the world underwent enforced isolation, I found myself in familiar if sequestered territory.

KATE RECOMMENDS ───────────────

Gian Lorenzo Bernini, *Mattress for sleeping figure*, Villa Borghese, Rome, 1620; Jericho Brown, *The Tradition* (Picador); Jim Carruth, *Killochries* (Freight Books); Hélène Cixous, *Dream I Tell You*, trans. Beverley Bie Brahic (Columbia University Press); Peter Davidson, *The Last of the Light* (Reaktion); John Donne, *Devotions upon Emergent Occasions*; Doireann Ní Ghríofa, *A Ghost in the Throat* (forthcoming from Tramp Press 2020); Louise Glück, *Faithful and Virtuous Night* (Carcanet); Maggie Nelson, *Bluets* (Cape); Virgina Woolf, *On Being Ill* (Paris Press); Rachel Whiteread, *Shallow breath 1988*, Tate exhibition 2017.

I RECOMMENDATION

...My bed's an island
where I've *cried to dream again*

Image: Zephyr Penoyre

THE LONG BEDS

When we look out at dawn
across the shipyard, rafts are being fetched
            by tugs, and on the rafts whole families have slept
                              out in the cool,

            grand old dynastic families in white,
    the women's faces veiled. Motionless
            and queenly in repose, they're surely only playing dead?

Past floats
    one part-unwrapped young person with a lovely face,
                big eyes perhaps I recognise. In girlhood
        wasn't she my closest friend?

                    Meanwhile attendants rouse the men-folk
        bringing cups. And all the time the sea, dull green,
                        laps at their long beds hanging in the water.

NINA MINGYA POWLES

Nina Mingya Powles is a writer and zinemaker from Aotearoa New Zealand, living in London. She is the author of *Luminescent* (Seraph Press, 2017), a set of four poetry pamphlets, and *Tiny Moons*, a food memoir (The Emma Press, 2020). She is the founding editor of the small press Bitter Melon 苦瓜 which publishes limited-edition, risograph printed poetry pamphlets and poem broadsides by poets from the Asian diaspora.

MAGNOLIA, 木蘭

NINE ARCHES PRESS | £9.99 | PBS PRICE £7.50

Magnolia, 木蘭 is a tour-de-force collection which roves effortlessly between languages, cultures and places, and between the actual and the imagined. One of its many rewards is the way in which it explores ambiguity and the proliferation of meaning – "this moment when the dream and the real begin to blur" – with absolute assurance and clarity.

"There are many things I am trying to hold together", announces the speaker in 'Field Notes on a Downpour'. Later she goes on, "Certain languages contain more kinds of rain than others, and I have eaten them all." Clouds are a leitmotif, from the smog of Shanghai to the first character of "my mother's name" which can mean "multicoloured clouds", to Ella Yelich-O'Connor's description of synaesthesia as "clouds of coloured gas moving slowly closer and then away".

The in-between spaces this collection explores are rich, transformative, and endlessly generative: the sophistication of what is being articulated matched seamlessly by a fluent and commanding language (or rather languages). Whether in denser, prose-poem form, or in poems which fully exploit the power of white space to amplify the resonance of islanded words, Powles' formal range and risk is evidenced everywhere.

Films and food are equal highlights. 'Watching Mulan in Chinese with English subtitles' provides an unforgettable opening, while descriptions of Shanghai specialities, lovingly assembled, are some of the most memorable (and hunger-inducing) descriptions of food in poetry I know:

> Tip the plump yolk of each duck egg into tiny bowls.
> Place one on top of the bed of sticky rice, a row of suns

Throughout *Magnolia,* 木蘭 the proliferation of such acutely realised detail makes us believe in everything – even dreams, rain and clouds – and even if that "everything" is still so fragile and complex it might "collapse at the slightest touch."

> between metal and skin between clouds of steam
> between touch and   the possibility of touch
> the body of a downpour caught in halogen light

SINÉAD MORRISSEY

NINA MINGYA POWLES

Magnolia, 木蘭 is a title that contains layers of meaning. This will be obvious to any Chinese speakers: "Mùlán" (木蘭) means magnolia, which is also the official flower of the city of Shanghai, where I wrote most of these poems. I spent a year and a half in Shanghai studying Mandarin. It's one of several places in the world that I call home, and I always knew that one day I would have to write a "Shanghai book" but I didn't know what form it would take. The end result is partly a collection of love letters to Shanghai, but it's also about loneliness, and about trying to retrace my steps back towards a lost language. In 2018 I moved to London and I had this scattered pile of poems, dream-fragments, and essay pieces that I'd begun writing in Shanghai. I set to work finishing the drafts and began to see some kind of collection taking shape. 'Girl warrior, or: watching Mulan (1998) in Chinese with English subtitles' is both the first poem in the book and the oldest poem in the book. It's special to me because, unlike almost everything else I've written, it hasn't changed very much from the first draft, which came out all at once. At the time, I was part of a poetry group who ran open-mic nights at bars around Shanghai. The first time I shared this poem was at a weird craft beer bar on the ground floor of a big luxury fashion mall. Writing 'Girl warrior' gave me a starting point from which I could explore things like language, dialect, and being mixed, through the medium of poetry.

> When I watch *Mulan* in Chinese with English subtitles / I understand only some of the words
>
> My focus shifts to certain details / how Mulan drags a very large cannon across the snow / with very small wrists
>
> how the villain has skin as dark as coal / and such small eyes / he has no irises
>
> once a guy told me mixed girls are the most beautiful / because they aren't really white / but they aren't really Asian either

NINA RECOMMENDS

Two books that contain journeys into (and away from) other languages are *States of the Body Produced by Love* by Nisha Ramayya (Ignota Books) and *Chronology* by Zahra Patterson (Ugly Duckling Presse). Both engage with colonialism, myth and femininity. Two pamphlets I've recently loved are *Translation is a Mode=Translation is an Anti-Neocolonial Mode* (Ugly Duckling Presse), a treatise by Don Mee Choi on poetry translation as a feminist, anti-colonial practice; and *Doing the Most with the Least* by Momtaza Mehri (Goldsmiths Press).

RECOMMENDATION

THE GREAT WALL (2016)

When Matt Damon saved China
        by driving his spear into the alien's mouth

I was distracted by Lin Mei's long braided hair
        and the way she holds herself so still

ready to strike down her enemies
        with a knife in each fist

but some things are fixed
        in the white-saviour narrative

like the exotic love interest who will risk everything
        as ancient cities crumble around her

and when you asked me what I thought
        afterwards in the autumn rain

I wanted to say *some parts were beautiful*
        like the pagoda of iridescent glass

shattering into pieces of pink and blue light
        just as Lin Mei lets loose her arrow

and also when you whispered something
        in my ear and I was hit by the shockwave

caused by my body and your breath existing
        in the same moment in the same universe

Image: Kerry Ann Lee

months later you told me you cried during *Rogue One*
    the scene where two men hold each other

weeping beneath the palm trees and light beams
    blasting the leaves apart and their hands

shaking moments before a star-destroying weapon
    obliterates their small wrecked portion of universe

I didn't know what to do with these space-opera feelings
    only that I had to exit this particular narrative

in which our knees are just touching
    and we are laughing while the city disappears around us

as if we could reach back through hyperspace
    to touch the silver holograms of our past selves

as if we could go back to some other time
    on some other planet

before the first particles of energy let go of themselves
    like the thousand paper lanterns

released into the sky above the Great Wall
    a thousand tiny fires trapped inside

NINA MINGYA POWLES

27

MERVYN TAYLOR

Mervyn Taylor, a longtime Brooklyn resident, was born in Belmont, on the island of Trinidad. He has taught at Bronx Community College, The New School University, and in the NYC public school system. The author of several books of poetry, including *No Back Door* (2010), *The Waving Gallery* (2014), *Voices Carry* (2017), and the CD *Road Clear*, with bassist David Williams, he currently serves on the advisory board of Slapering Hol Press, Hudson Valley.

COUNTRY OF WARM SNOW

SHEARSMAN | £10.95 | PBS PRICE £8.22

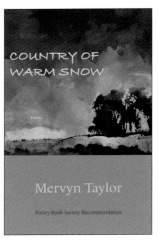

For those of us who teach, one of the things we might find ourselves imploring our writing students to do is to "pay attention" to the life of things all around them; in Taylor's new collection, we have an exemplar to give them. The opening poem 'Status' is an important poem to begin with, considering as it does the differing identities and hierarchies which might exist societally, politically, in work, but most importantly questioning what the status of the poet, or the speaker of the poem, might be within the observed scene as well, a question which this collection returns to again and again.

> ...I have no idea what
> his status is. I only know that when
> I stand before the
> mirror, my old suit
>
> looks new, and that I would hide him
> in my house, and feed him...

This is an immensely readable, heartfelt and moving collection, giving us the stories of real people, often kept at the artificial margins of narratives they don't control. Layers of time fold over each other, unsettling childhood memory, exile and immigration, gentrification and the attempted erasure of the old (which the poem can try to preserve), poets and writers who we've lost (Toni Morrison, Derek Walcott). In one memorable poem of a barber carrying on working whilst gun battles and gang violence happen outside, we see glimpses of the lives being lived just to the left of the newspaper headline.

> Under some rickety stairs
> Hassam cuts hair, he and his
> customers ducking when
> they hear gunfire.

The "warm snow" referenced in the title turns up part-way through the book, and comes to symbolise, perhaps, thwarted expectation, the jarring reality of things experienced for the first time in a new place, and ultimately of things which might seem one way until we're in them, until the reality of them becomes clear. There is real warmth and humour in these poems, and such heart; like the gallery guard who takes the focus away from great masterpieces in one poem, everyday people are elevated here, and given the status, quite rightly, of art.

ANDREW McMILLAN

MERVYN TAYLOR

I'm thrilled no end that my new book, *Country of Warm Snow*, has been chosen as a Poetry Book Society Recommendation. When I first sent the manuscript to Shearsman Books in 2018, I was disappointed to hear that the earliest publication date would be in 2020. Now, in hindsight, I'm happy for the delay. Over time, the collection has changed, although the original concept and direction have remained true. In one way or another, all of my six previous books have been wrestling with the same theme – a life lived in two countries, led by the physical presence in one, and the emotional, dreamstate attachment to the other. A perfect metaphor for this might be those foreday mornings, asleep at home on Ocean Ave, Brooklyn, when a friend who worked the early shift at the airport would stop at the intersection just below my window, and, while his car idled, turn up the volume of his CD player, blasting some old Sparrow or Kitchener calypso he knew would join us both in recognition, especially if it was a morning deep in winter, below freezing.

This collection, unlike my others, is not subdivided into sections seeking to accommodate Brooklyn and Port of Spain, as if acknowledging the thousands of miles, snowdrifts versus heat, Carnival among tall buildings and steelbands begging a lodging, as one poem says. I think, like the tailors of Belmont, the verses have finally stitched the countries together, moving between territories, contiguous, each taking up where the other left off. The title is taken from a note by the outsider artist, Josep Baqué, describing a piece of his work: "Interior of some marvelous large islands at two million meters above sea level, unexplored, uninhabitable by civilized beings, a country of warm snow." The poems acknowledge the ordinary lives of the inhabitants of these islands, their daily struggle to retain some semblance of dignity. The book is dedicated to my father, who, whether in his uniform as a railway conductor, or with the goats he took to minding, pulling him down the street, kept an enduring sense of self, while saying very little. I hope I speak for him.

MERVYN RECOMMENDS

I'd like to recommend these writers whose work I've held in high regard over the years: *Dead Shark on the N Train*, by Susana H. Case (Broadstone Books), a complex tracing of the penchant for violence in relationships through personal reflection and the examination of recreated crime scenes from the work of Frances Glessner Lee. *The Migrant States*, Indran Amirthanayagam (Hanging Loose Press) which includes extraordinary poems for the anniversary of Walt Whitman on what would have been the poet's 200th birthday. *No Small Gift*, Jennifer Franklin (Four Way Books) by a poet with the gift of gratitude in the face of enormous challenges, who offers strategies for survival in poems that are nuanced and lovely.

Blue skies turning red for years

COUNTRY OF WARM SNOW

For Courtney

You stopped by, feet swollen
from sleeping sitting up. When
I think of how we entered this city,

separating through the streets
in the months after, I picture the
state you had gotten lost in, east,

west, perhaps one of the dry
ones, like Nevada. Never afraid
to dream, your idea of America

remained what we'd seen in the
movies: fields where men keep
rounding the bases, cheeks red

with October chill. That first winter,
you said the snow looked warm.
And, now someone's promised you

a cot in a basement, you grin with
delight, as if the offer has redeemed
whatever wrong was done to you.

Image: Tony Ward

GERÐUR KRISTNÝ

Gerður Kristný was brought up in Reykjavík and graduated in French and Comparative Literature from the University of Iceland. She has published poetry, short stories, novels and books for children, and a biography *Myndin af pabba – Saga Thelmu* (*A Portrait of Dad – Thelma's Story*) for which she won the Icelandic Journalism Award in 2005. Other awards for her work include the Children's Choice Book Prize in 2003 for *Marta Smarta* (*Smart Martha*), and the Halldór Laxness Literary Award in 2004 for her novel *Bátur með segli og allt* (*A Boat With a Sail and All*). Her collection of poetry, *Höggstaður* (*Soft Spot*), was nominated for the Icelandic Literature Prize in 2007 which she later won in 2010 for her poetry book *Blóðhófnir* (*Bloodhoof*). In 2018, Arc published her collection *Drápa* (*A Reykjavik Murder Mystery*), translated by Rory McTurk, in a bilingual edition.

Rory McTurk graduated from Oxford and the University of Iceland, Reykjavík. He has taught at the universities of Lund, Copenhagen, University College, Dublin, and Leeds. He is the author of several critical works including *Studies in Ragnars Saga Loðbrókar and its Major Scandinavian Analogues*, *Chaucer and the Norse and Celtic Worlds*, *The Blackwell Companion to Old Norse-Icelandic Literature and Culture*, as well as numerous essays, articles and translations.

SÁLUMESSA: REYKJAVIK REQUIEM

ARC PUBLICATIONS | £10.99 | PBS PRICE £8.25

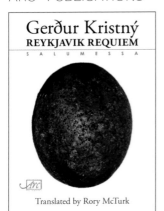

The Special Commendation always feels as though it should go to a book outside of the realms of the traditional single volume collection; perhaps it could be an anthology, or a selected poems, and in this case an astonishing narrative poem from Gerður Kristný, translated from the Icelandic by Rory McTurk. As the introduction from Sigþrúður Gunnarsdóttir tells us, this is the third in a trilogy of poetic sequences on the themes of oppression and violence against women, looking at the story of a woman who was abused as a child in a small Icelandic village. The Icelandic appears, page by page, aligned to the opposite side of the English translation, first on the left and then on the right, so the reader is constantly thrown between the two languages.

Your childhood a lake
frozen to its depths

By now you had
crushed off
the ice around you

shaken off
its frail hold

No-one
was to suffer
the same
as you

The pared-back, distilled language pulls us through a terrifying and utterly gripping narrative, the white space around each of the brief windows of text feels desolate, like an empty, unsettling landscape. Part of the dazzling accomplishment of this book is its ability to both hold the reader, by giving them the details of plot, movement and inner-voice one might expect from a novel, whilst also being able to give us the precise lyric glimpse which feels unique to poetry. This is a quite remarkable book, which we felt deserved this Special Commendation accolade. Never shy about its own violence, never looking away and not afraid to leave us in the snow-white silence that exists between the two languages on the page. A shout-out too for Rory McTurk, whose translation here deserves equal plaudits.

ANDREW McMILLAN

SELECTOR'S COMMENT

REYKJAVIK REQUIEM

Hún horfir
í gegnum
íshelluna
sem bróðirinn
steypti henni

Nývöknuð
inn í draum
sem hún velur
hvernig endar

She gazes
through the floe
of ice
which her brother
moulded for her

Newly awakened
into a dream
the end of which
she chooses

WORLD CHOICE: I AM A ROHINGYA
EDITED BY JAMES BYRNE AND SHEHZAR DOJA
ARC PUBLICATIONS | £9.99 | PBS PRICE £7.50

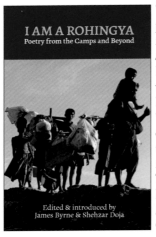

I AM A ROHINGYA
Poetry from the Camps and Beyond

Edited & introduced by
James Byrne & Shehzar Doja

"To make rhymes out of gunshots, / To make poetry out of death and destruction, / This heart of mine is not skilled enough," writes Yar Tin in *I am a Rohingya* a book that collects voices from Cox's Bazaar, the oldest and largest refugee camps in the world. Cox's Bazaar began in 1797 when Captain Hiram Cox assigned "wastelands" to thousands of "refugees". The people who live here are Rohingya, one of the most persecuted ethnic minorities on the planet. They live in camps that are so crowded many can't even get in. But, somehow, poets do. They ask questions: "What do you feel", Maung Hla Shwe asks, "when you see your sibling's corpse / inside a mass grave?" And here, in lines by Zaki Ovais from inside the camps:

I'm a fly in the kitchen, buzzing
on the boundary of a blind wall.

I'm a chicken under mother's wing,
confined to the narrows of a wattle.

I'm a dove on the street of Yangon,
jailed in the cage of inhumanity

I'm the water flowing in Mayu river,
missing my partner – Air.

I'm a human in the universe,
denied the most basic rights.
I'm someone I'm afraid of.

In making this inaugural selection for the Poetry Book Society's World Choice, which aims to honour an outstanding work of Non-European poetry or translation from the last five years, I especially considered the history of how *I am a Rohingya* came to be: Shehzar Doja, a Bangladeshi/French poet, and James Byrne, a British poet, came to Cox's Bazaar to work with twenty refugees. So this book is the direct result of the first writing collective on record ever facilitated in the camps, since 1797. According to the editors of this book, they "quickly realized that the poets gathered in the room weren't just *making* history by being part of the poetry collective, they wanted to *mark* history."

ILYA KAMINSKY

MY LIFE BY PACIFIST FAROOQ

Here's my life in brief...

I was a frog in a well,
A prisoner in the jail of fresh air.
In the dark, dark cosmos,
No days, just nights, nights.

A small cormorant survives
the genocidal waves
by being flung, crashing
into the world's strangeness.

Storm of racism, of hate –
This is my life.

Just like an action movie
In which you are the gangster.
Just like an actor who cannot discover his lines.

In Arakan, they kill and bury you
under the treasure of human rights.

TEN CONTEMPORARY SPANISH WOMEN POETS
TRANSLATED AND EDITED BY TERENCE DOOLEY
SHEARSMAN | £12.95 | PBS PRICE £9.72

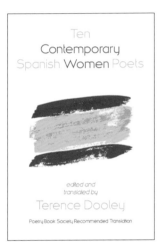

Ten poets herein belong to the first generation that didn't live in the shadow of Franco's dictatorship, though its political echo is still here: Martha Asunción Alonso speaks of "a nation of sleep-walkers" who "had sweated all their country's blood." These lines resonate especially for our own crisis in the English-speaking world. Reading, one is overwhelmed by the larger historical crisis, but delighted by the abundance of private lyric voices. Works like Erika Martínez's marvellous 'Seeing Through' stay in memory long after the poem ends.

> First. I collect keys
> because a lot of people trust me
> and their trust is a pillow
> on which all I could never do
> rests its head.
>
> Second. I collect keys
> because I have several selves
> since I squeezed through the crack
> in my work horizon
> travelling far and wide
> on urgent but possibly
> futile errands.
>
> Third. I collect keys
> because their heft in my pocket calms
> my all-encompassing revealing fear
> of being locked out...

Here, too, is a fragment from Miriam Reyes:

> Will you teach me to live?
> I'll let you touch my collection of shells
> I'll share with you the nail-clippings I keep in my pockets.
> ...The promised land is for other people.
> For us sand-dunes:
> country that alters with the wind.

The polyphony of these ten voices both challenges and refreshes; it allows us to see all the doors that had been closed for generations of women, and also "the next doors they'll open".

ILYA KAMINSKY

THREE BOOKS BY MESÁNDEL VIRTUSIO ARGUELLES
TRANSLATED BY KRISTINE ONG MUSLIM
BROKEN SLEEP BOOKS | £11.99 | PBS PRICE £9.00

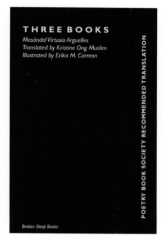

THREE BOOKS
Mesándel Virtusio Arguelles
Translated by Kristine Ong Muslim
Illustrated by Erika M. Carreon

POETRY BOOK SOCIETY RECOMMENDED TRANSLATION

Broken Sleep Books

The Philippines is a multi-lingual state with over one hundred and seventy living languages. English and Spanish were official colonial languages, and it was not until well into the 20th Century that Filipino was proclaimed the national language. Although Mesándel Virtusio Arguelles's beautiful lyric fragments never refer to this history directly, it lurks behind the work of these erasure poems:

> In court
> being sworn is not being sworn
>
> not being sworn
> not being sworn
>
> not
> permitted
> —
> Be a rock
> to withstand
> the stench, smoke

Mesándel Virtusio Arguelles is the kind of poet who investigates the public speech (language of movie titles, popular political memoirs, etc.) to find a strange lyricism:

> So it begins – foam
> in the mouth. Fraught liason
> with the bed's web.

This excavation of public language offers a sudden tonality that's both sharp and delicate, an example of how metaphysics is hiding in plain sight, everywhere.

THE POET & TRANSLATOR

Mesándel Virtusio Arguelles's works and interests encompass conceptual writing, translation, film and video, installation, found objects, and text-based experimentation. A recipient of multiple national awards in the Philippines, Arguelles is the author of twenty books of and about poetry. He teaches Literature and Creative Writing at the De La Salle University in Manila.

Kristine Ong Muslim is a translator and author of nine books, including the poetry collections *Lifeboat* (University of Santo Tomas), *Meditations of a Beast* (Cornerstone Press) and *Black Arcadia* (University of the Philippines Press).

ILYA KAMINSKY

CHERYL PEARSON

Cheryl Pearson is the author of *Menagerie*, a pamphlet of poems with illustrations by Amy Evans, published by The Emma Press. Cheryl's first poetry collection, *Oysterlight*, was published by Pindrop Press in 2017, and she is the winner of the 2016 Cheshire Prize for Literature, the 2017 Torbay Poetry Competition, and was Highly Commended in the Costa Short Story Awards 2017. She lives in Manchester and spends her free time in the Peak District where she can usually be found climbing hills or drinking beer. She is currently working on a short story collection.

MENAGERIE BY CHERYL PEARSON

THE   EMMA   PRESS | £10.00 |

Menagerie just works as a pamphlet. It holds an element of surprise. There is something of a child's wisdom. As stated in 'Hermit', "a poem is an egg with a horse inside". The craft is well tempered. We are invited into worlds that seem familiar and yet they are rendered new. With all that is going on outside in our daily lives the author holds our attention from cover to cover. It would be unfair to call this a cluster of nature poems, even when the author divides the pamphlet into three sections of water, earth and air. However, with that crude categorisation I notice that after reading this pamphlet I observed the world differently. In her poem 'A Comb Jellyfish Swallows Another Comb Jellyfish' we enter the world through light:

> You see now how light travels. How language travels.
> Like the lick of flame in an air balloon's silk. Illumination
> from the inside out, a snake with its tail in the plug of its mouth.
> How *swallow* turns in. How in consuming, is also consumed.
> An open throat like a chimney full of sky, a pouring in
> of light drunk in by light...

The above poem is from the water section. Light acts as the universal binding agent in all sections of the book.

> EARTH
> 'Hedgehog'
> Milk on flat moon comes
> at dusk.
>
> AIR
> 'Flamingo'
> ...that other light
> that burns, and cannot be extinguished.

Pearson uses her musings on eighteen creatures to gesture towards the wider world. This *Menagerie* is for our display. Its purpose is two-fold, first she primes our curiosity and then she interrogates the way that we gaze. For example when she renders the 2014 public dissection of Marius the giraffe at Copenhagen Zoo in front an audience that included a class of school children.

MARIUS

*In 2014, Marius, a young giraffe at Copenhagen
Zoo, was deemed unsuitable for breeding and
euthanised, before being publicly dissected.
Onlookers included a group of schoolchildren.*

Laid out flat like a flag, or hunter's rug,
a human peg at each steaming corner.

*See the heart which measures half a metre.
The black tongue.* The kneeling children

lean in closer. Perhaps by now he'd be
bones on the plain. Hyena. Matchstick-

leg snapped clean. Perhaps he'd be
an hour older. The sky's a wound. *Look,*

says a keeper. His red hand dips to the gut
then flowers. *His last supper. Bread. Rye.*

In the corner, bluebottles tread a bucket
of parts. Already the acacia leaves are dry.

RACHEL LONG is a poet and founder of the Octavia Poetry Collective for Womxn of Colour, which is housed at Southbank Centre, in London. Rachel's poetry and prose have been published widely, most recently in *Filigree, Mal* and *The White Review*. Since 2015 she has been Assistant Tutor to Jacob Sam-La Rose on The Barbican Young Poets programme.

JAIL LETTER

All Saturday I sit viced between Mum's legs.
When it's dark and all my friends are inside she says,
Finished! like 'Ta-dah!' as if anything about this has been quick
or thrilling.

The corners of my eyes have been stitched into my hairline.
All the 'sheep's wool' they love to touch and say eww to at school
has been harvested into rows at the top of my head;
black crown or web.

'Mum, my scalp burns!'
'Ungrateful! Look at you, beautiful as Winnie Mandela!'
I don't know who this is,
but it doesn't sound like someone Ben Clark will fancy.

MY DARLING FROM THE LIONS

PICADOR | £10.99 | PBS PRICE £8.25

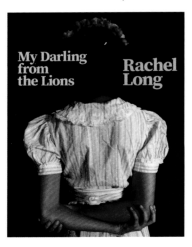

Some of the questions central to Rachel Long's debut *My Darling from the Lions* form a sharp and unrelenting satire which connects both mind and body to place. How subjects pertaining to desire, womanhood, race and other cultural normalcies engender an anxiety associated with the lyric subject – the ways it can be imagined to exist in the mind of others. Much of the work occupies several spaces at once, endowing it with a rich, multifaceted propensity, such as at the close of the poem 'Hotel Art, Barcelona', "You lift my dress. I shoulder-width my legs, / is love not this? – gripping a fence in the sky." A tapestry of lyric and anti-lyric.

References to standardised ideals of beauty in relation to the body are a common motif throughout Long's work. The poem 'Apples' wrestles with a discomforting duality; moving through a series of controlled narratives which constantly turn to invoke a sense of bifurcation:

> Last night, I missed my train by seconds.
> So close that one part of me did catch it
> and waved from the window to the other half
> still panting on the platform...

The piece, peppered with comic and poignant imagery, "I am magazine educated, so have known for a while / that my body is an apple" along with quotidian micro aggressions which undermine the speaker, "I bruise so easy I worry it's leukaemia. / *No*, the doctor says, again, *it's just your dark skin*. / She recommends scar serum", signals in part towards the performative or spurious nature of white liberalism. Long establishes throughout the collection her lateral skill as a poet, one who is equipped to grapple with an array of complex subject matters. The writing with its wit and charm is underpinned by a constant unease which manages to couple grand theory with anecdote and introspection in a way that appears realised and coherent.

> ...I fell asleep in the chair
> with my head back,
> my arms tight at my sides.
> I say, *What, like bracing for impact?*
> He says, *No, like working something out
> with the sky.*

| SELECTOR'S COMMENT ANTHONY ANAXAGOROU

RACHEL LONG

*My Darling from the Lion*s is a narrative collection in three parts which threads experiences of the learning and unlearning of shame, the body, sex, faith, Blackness, lineage, prophecy and healing.

The title is taken from Psalm 35, v. 17 of the King James version of the Bible (the only version according to my mother), "Lord, how long wilt thou look on? rescue my soul from their destructions, my darling from the lions." The verse makes me ache. I think it's the preciousness of "my darling", and more so in the regarding and naming oneself a darling. Imagine!

I'd constantly call out at night because of the dark, a bad dream, something walking in the walls. I had a good imagination. Sometimes it ate me. My Dad would often come and coax me, claim there were no such thing as dancing ghost ferrets; no, I couldn't catch the Black Death from a reading a book about the Black Death; the shadows were just X, Y, go to sleep! Dad would set a timer on his running watch. I'd be coaxed for as long as it took him to run 800 metres. Then I'd be left. As he was leaving, he'd put on a Disney sing-along cassette for me. Bambi's mum was shot on that tape every night. Like, actual hunter rifle gunshots followed by some ragged classical music to suggest her running for her life, then Bambi crying slow tempo with all the leaves of the forest swishing. I have no idea why I never said, please don't put that tape on. Maybe I did, eventually.

It was always Dad who came until Mum did. When she padded down the corridor you knew you were in for it. But sometimes she'd just lay a hand on my forehead and pray for me, for my protection. I would always be able to sleep after she did, a precious sleep. Like I'd been allowed to keep a light on.

This book is about the ways my mum protected me. It is about a girl scared of morphing lions; eating, dying, the church, men. It is about growing up in fear but also wetting-yourself-laughing with friends. There is loss and learning and loving and finding.

RACHEL RECOMMENDS

Patricia Smith, *Incendiary Art* (Bloodaxe); Kei Miller, *In Nearby Bushes* (Carcanet); Caroline Bird, *The Air Year* (Carcanet); Gboyega Odubanjo, *While I Yet Live* (Bad Betty Press) and Audre Lorde, *Your Silence Will Not Protect You* (Silver Press).

I WILD CARD CHOICE

AUTUMN BOOK REVIEWS

Memory, in Romalyn Ante's enchanting debut, is alive and vivid. Travelling between the Philippines and the UK, this collection explores ideas of belonging and culture. Storytelling lies at the heart of these poems, stories that gain new significance as they cross generations and continents, new stories forged by new beginnings that nevertheless reflect the voices of the past. These poems are rich in history but unsentimental, playful in form but grounded in reality. A wonderful collection, it asks what it means to be home.

JULY | CHATTO | £10.00 | PBS PRICE £7.50

──────── SUMITA CHAKRABORTY: ARROW ────────

This recent winner of the Forward Prize for Best Single Poem summons forth breathless visions and sonorous prophecies in a wry and dazzling oracular collection. Chakraborty "arrows from times of grief" and the death of a sister to micro-theses on daily existence. Drawing on sources as various as Hesiod's *Theogony*, Brigit Pegeen Kelly, *Moby Dick*, Nina Simone and Rilke, this is an awe-inspiring, soaring debut; both epic and distilled.

SEPTEMBER | CARCANET | £10.99 | PBS PRICE £8.25

──────── SARAH CROSSAN: HERE IS THE BEEHIVE ────────

Crossan's *Here is the Beehive* is a novel in free verse, a compelling and tragic story of an affair between lawyer and client. Thoroughly captivating, both sordid and profound, this is a powerful read concerned with ideas of responsibility and the allure of the forbidden, the limitless complexity of relationships, and the strange and damaging ways in which we explore our emotional responses to the people in our lives.

AUGUST | BLOOMSBURY | £12.99 (HB) | PBS PRICE £9.75

JONATHAN DAVIDSON: A COMMONPLACE
APPLES, BRICKS AND OTHER PEOPLE'S POEMS

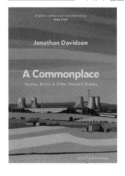

Jonathan Davidson gathers a commonplace of poems to offer solace and inspiration. *Apples, Bricks and Other People's Poems* opens up a lively conversation about how poetry is made and exists in the everyday. Davidson's own poems spanning from Lisbon to Nicaragua, sit alongside sixteen other poets, including Maura Dooley, Jackie Kay and Zaffar Kunial, and the poet's reflections on each. This is an inspirational shared experience of poetries in dialogue, which restores our sense of poetry community.

AUGUST | SMITH | DOORSTOP | £9.95 | PBS PRICE £7.47

JORIE GRAHAM: RUNAWAY

Pulitzer Prize winner Jorie Graham is one of America's most distinguished living poets; a vital voice for our age of ecological and social disaster. *Runaway* prophesises a dystopian "deep future" where the sky no longer exists and "on the screen / in the screen / you die". Here too are love songs to the pre or post-human, '[to] the last [be] human', which urge us to listen: "The earth said / remember me. / The earth said / don't let go". We ignore her at our peril.

SEPTEMBER | CARCANET | £12.99 | PBS PRICE £9.75

ACCURSED POETS: DISSIDENT POETRY FROM SOVIET RUSSIA
EDITED AND TRANSLATED BY ANATOLY KUDRYAVITSKY

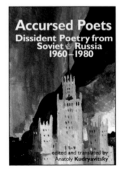

Accursed Poets: Dissident Poetry from Soviet Russia 1960-1980 anthologises a phenomenal amount of 20th Century poetry from dissidents, the censored, and the marginalised within Soviet Russia. A unique work of historical and literary significance, this bilingual edition comprises the works of over fifteen poets, and includes an illuminating introduction by the translator and editor, Anatoly Kudryavitsky.

OCTOBER | SMOKESTACK BOOKS | £8.99 | PBS PRICE £6.75

| BOOK REVIEWS

AUTUMN BOOK REVIEWS

─── MICHAEL LONGLEY: THE CANDLELIGHT MASTER ───

Michael Longley's latest collection encompasses a breadth of time with poems penned for familiar faces from history, art, literature and Greek mythology sitting alongside more personal dedications. He shares memories of primary school, time with old friends, and family held dear as he reflects on turning eighty. You can feel the sincerity in every poem, and by his own word, Michael Longley is "the candlelight master / Striking a match in the shadows".

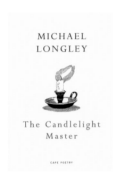

MICHAEL LONGLEY

The Candlelight Master

CAPE POETRY

AUGUST | CAPE | £10.00 | PBS PRICE £7.50

─── PASCALE PETIT: TIGER GIRL ───

This spellbinding collection draws upon Petit's Indian heritage in an ode to her grandmother, "the tiger girl... who keeps a jungle folded in her greenhouse". Petit's own visits to Madhya Pradesh inspire mythic jungles where men sew owl's eyes shut, women wear fire and empress tigresses "leap to extinction". Full of all the wonder and horror of the world, *Tiger Girl* questions "what is the mastery that makes us / drive other races, other species, to extinction?" These are urgent eco-poems which "sing the songs that burn / at the centre of the earth".

SEPTEMBER | BLOODAXE | £10.99 | PBS PRICE £8.25

─── RIBKA SIBHATU: AULÒ! AULÒ! AULÒ! ───
TRANSLATED BY ANDRÉ NAFFIS-SAHELY

In 1979, aged seventeen, Ribka Sibhatu was sentenced to prison for criticising the Eritrean government, the memory of which resurfaces in a moving elegy to a friend who died in prison. Now living in exile in Italy, writing in Italian, Tigrinya and Amharic, three of her five languages or "stepdaughters", this is a "multi-lingual lament". It is also a powerful act of witness and defiance as Shibatu recalls the 357 Eritrean refugees who drowned off the coast of Lampedusa and preserves native fables in "aulòs" or chant-poems which soar: "in exile / I sing of infinity".

JULY | PTC WORLD POET SERIES | £7.00 | PBS PRICE £5.25

SASHA STEENSEN: EVERY THING AWAKE

This is a collection preoccupied with sleep; sleep both as biological process and a folkloric symbol, insomnia and sleep restriction therapy. Steensen meanders through different states of consciousness. She navigates the passage of time, through observations of infancy, childhood, and parenthood. *Every Thing Awake's* pages are filled with imaginative, dreamlike verse.

AUGUST | SHEARSMAN | £10.95 | PBS PRICE £8.22

MARIA TAYLOR: DRESSING FOR THE AFTERLIFE

Running, ageing, loving, living, loss and a glamorous stream of silent movie stars combine to create this resolute, defiant, humorous and incredibly moving collection of poems. As a runner of a certain age I loved Maria Taylor's final poem of the collection 'Woman Running Alone' – it really lifted me. She has a brilliant eye for the detail of the everyday – situations that are recognisable but rendered so imaginatively with a mix of humour, pathos and boldness.

SEPTEMBER | NINE ARCHES PRESS | £9.99 | PBS PRICE £7.50

SEAN O'BRIEN: IT SAYS HERE

This new collection by Forward and T.S. Eliot prize winner Sean O'Brien centres around 'Hammersmith', a cinematic sequence about post-war England, "a history they could not know was taking place". O'Brien examines the "poisoned well" of Englishness, class and politics: "The world for which the nation fought admits / No Blacks and no dogs and no Irish". But this is so much more than a searing social history, it is "the history of an imagination" which narrates us all into being: "What am I but the tale / You did not think that you were telling?"

SEPTEMBER | PICADOR | £10.99 | PBS PRICE £8.25

BOOK REVIEWS

AUTUMN PAMPHLETS

TROY CABIDA: WAR DOVE

An absorbing debut from the London-based Filipino poet Troy Cabida, *War Dove* follows a journey to self-understanding and acceptance, navigating profound tensions within the subject and in relation to others. This moving, thoughtful chronicle of identity, the experience of being an outsider, and the importance of exploring and embracing one's nature, is enriched by snippets of Tagalog running deftly throughout Cabida's verse.

BAD BETTY PRESS | £6.00 |

ARJI MANUELPILLAI : MUTTON ROLLS

At first Manuelpillai's verse is effortlessly casual, conversational, and intimate. The poet's voice jumps from the page. With a swift turn it moves into a different mode; something altogether more anarchic and acerbic. *Mutton Rolls* is striking and dizzying, at once humorous and poignant. Probing, unflinching explorations of identities and race, the relationship between tradition and metropolitan modernity, jostle for space within this excellent debut.

OUTSPOKEN PRESS | £7.00 |

PRATYUSHA: BULBUL CALLING

This limited-edition pamphlet by the Indo-Swiss poet Pratyusha is an exquisite hand-sewn and illustrated risograph. Full of fragments and feverish heat, *Bulbul Calling* slips between Tamil, German and English; shifting psycho-geographies, "along the Rhine I found both tongue and / apparition / *unbeständig* / where is the absence"; and defiant utterance: "refugee, immigrant expat; all moneyed apart... our true witness is with our names: / speak, Pratyusha, of everything, at the shore".

BITTER MELON PRESS 苦瓜 | £7.00 |

BEN RAY: THE KINDNESS OF THE EEL

A winner of the 2019 New Poets Prize as judged by Mary Jean Chan, *The Kindness of the Eel* draws tales from the margins of history. Nestled within these pages is the story of the "Irish Giant" Charles Byrne, of a washed-up modern-day druid, of the bee-hives which survived the disastrous Notre Dame fire. There is a darkness to these poems; a watery sensibility which pulls you into Ray's world of quiet, compelling verse.

POETRY   BUSINESS | £5.00 |

JACQUELINE SAPHRA: VERITAS: POEMS AFTER ARTEMISIA

Recent Forward Prize shortlistee Jacqueline Saphra presents a series of ekphrastic poems alongside full colour reproductions of Artemisia Gentileschi's seventeenth century paintings. *Veritas* reframes art history to foreground Gentileschi's experience as a rape victim and paints a vivid portrait of the artist as a proto-feminist whose artwork "escapes an age of limits". Saphra fiercely interrogates the male gaze and the artistic canon to restore Gentileschi's much-neglected voice: "I'll pick my story".

HERCULES   EDITIONS | £10.00 |

JAY G YING: KATABASIS

Awarded the Poetry Business 2019 New Poets Prize, *Katabasis* descends into an underworld of war and grief. Inspired by the ancient Sumerian epic 'The Descent of Inanna' and modern day conflicts in Afghanistan, Ying combines formal experimentation and musicality to dramatic effect. *Katabasis* questions neo-colonial violence, "unmasked as an invader", and the uneasy balance of voyeurism and insight, "If I tell you where War is : What will / you give to me?"

POETRY   BUSINESS | £5.00 |

AUTUMN BOOK LISTINGS

AUTHOR	TITLE	PUBLISHER	RRP
Romalyn Ante	Antiemetic for Homesickness	Chatto & Windus	£10.00
Sean Ashton	Sampler	Valley Press	£12.00
Leah Atherton	A sky the colour of hope	Verve Poetry Press	£9.99
Ranald Barnicot	Friendship, Love, Abuse etc: Catullus Poems	Dempsey and Windle	£10.00
Fern Angel Beattie	The Art of Shutting Up	Broken Sleep Books	£8.00
Chris Beckett	Tenderfoot	Carcanet	£11.99
Erin Bolens	Alternate Endings	Burning Eye Books	£9.99
Sean Borodale	Inmates	Cape Poetry	£10.00
Carole Bromley	The Peregrine Falcons of York Minster	Valley Press	£10.99
Sumita Chakraborty	Arrow	Carcanet	£10.99
Eds. Jane Commane & Jacqueline Saphra	Primers Volume Five	Nine Arches Press	£9.99
Sarah Crossan	Here is the Beehive	Bloomsbury	£12.99
Jonathan Davidson	A Commonplace	The Poetry Business	£9.95
Kwame Dawes & John Kinsella	In The Name Of Our Families	Peepal Tree	£12.99
Ned Denny	B: After Dante	Carcanet	£16.99
Jennifer Firestone	Story	Ugly Duckling Presse	£15.00
Jon Glover	Birdsong on Mars	Carcanet	£11.99
Jorie Graham	Runaway	Carcanet	£12.99
Elise Hadgraft	Now There are no More Love Songs...	Verve Poetry Press	£9.99
Jeremy Hooker	Selected Poems 1965-2018	Shearsman	£14.95
Katherine Horrex	Growlery	Carcanet	£10.99
Jemima Hughes	Unorthodox	Verve Poetry Press	£9.99
Gerður Kristný	Reykjavik Requiem	Arc	12.99
Barbara Kingsolver	How To Fly (HB(	Faber	£14.99
Gregory Leadbetter	Maskwork	Nine Arches Press	£9.99
Rachel Levitsky	Neighbor	Ugly Duckling Presse	£14.00
Rachel Long	My Darling From the Lions	Picador	£10.99
Michael Longley	The Candlelight Master	Penguin Books	£10.00
Glynn Maxwell	How the Hell Are You	Picador	£10.99
James McDermott	MANATOMY	Burning Eye Books	£9.99
Kate Miller	The Long Beds	Carcanet	£10.99
Nina Mingya Powles	Magnolia, 木蘭	Nine Arches Press	£9.99
David Morley	FURY	Carcanet	£10.99
M.E. Muir	Ex Situ	Dempsey and Windle	£10.00
Sean O'Brien	It Says Here	Picador	£10.99
Nigel Pantling	It's Not Personal	The Poetry Business	£9.95
Simon Perril	The Slip	Shearsman	£10.95
Pascale Petit	Tiger Girl	Bloodaxe	£10.99
Ed. Cherry Potts	No Spider Harmed in the Making of this Book	Arachne	£9.99
Ian Seed	The Underground Cabaret	Shearsman	£10.95
Aidan Semmens	There Will Be Singing	Shearsman	£10.95
Di Slaney	Herd Queen	Valley Press	£12.00
Sasha Steensen	Every Thing Awake	Shearsman Books	£10.95
Phoebe Stuckes	Platinum Blonde	Bloodaxe	£9.95
Marc Swan	All it would take	tall-lighthouse	£10.00
Julian T. Brolaski	Gowanus Atropolis	Ugly Duckling Presse	£12.00
Maria Taylor	Dressing for the Afterlife	Nine Arches Press	£9.99
Mervyn Taylor	Country of Warm Snow	Shearsman	£10.95
Jeffrey Wainwright	As Best We Can	Carcanet	£10.99
Geoffrey Winch	Velocities and Drifts of Wind	Dempsey and Windle	£10.00
James Womack	Homunculus	Carcanet	£10.99
Various	The Forward Book of Poetry 2021	Faber	£9.99